Afternoon Abundance

Afternoon Abundance

poetry for wild souls

✦⁚

foster wilson

HARRINGTON HOUSE PRESS
LOS ANGELES

Harrington House Press
Los Angeles, CA

www.fosterwilson.com

ISBN: 979-8-9910358-0-4

Library of Congress Control Number: 2024914161

Illustrations and cover design by Suz Born
Author photo by Cesar Cardona

for my daughter, Emma
whose fire burns in every color

SPARK 1

BLAZE 23

EMBER 71

in the deepest darkest waters
where light and sound have drowned
lies the jewel of your truth
ready to surface for all to see

SPARK

this threshold has been crossed
and i feel the floodgates open
we earned this feeling
of running free
anything before me available
and i will ho d back nothing now

i wish the hands that hold this pen
could be invisible
for what i have to say is so dark
no one will see my light again
the freedom i crave
will make me callous in their eyes
it will be a witch hunt for my heart
a betrayal of the feminine
i am certain they will hang me
and strip me of my soul
left to suffocate slowly
from pity and disdain

i look at you
and i know your pain
i listen to you
and i feel your shame
i touch your skin
and i witness your hurt
and despite it all
you are still here

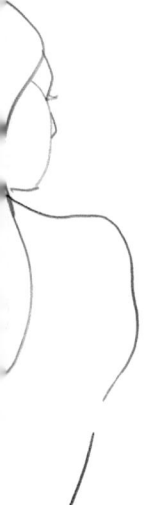

i bounce from one failure
to the next
with my eyes wide open
aware of the pain i'm causing
every step of the way
like undergoing surgery
without anesthesia
it confounds my senses
and strips my humanity
skin ripped off
tendons exposed
and mostly i think
i should flat line here
but i'm strapped to the table
and they keep resuscitating me

this monster in you
has a face i don't know
i can't see
how it got in you
your delicate hands
and soft skin
through what crack did it enter?
how did it pierce and infect you?
my love for you will not end
or halt or diminish
i will love you through this
but for now i am bruised
as i battle this beast in you
and in turn
also in me

i can't get clean
the tornado spins behind me
before i turn around
the dust is in my lungs
all this work
to cough it out
finally
i hit the ground

my head barely above the water's edge
i gasp for air
limbs sore with fatigue
exhausted
they churn while only my head manages
to touch the air
no body
the limbs and gut and core
are drowning
'but you are not dead' they say
just not dead
just for a moment, not dead
never alive
somewhere in between
and if you tire
you will fall into the dark abyss
because your reason for being here
was not enough
never enough
and so my legs work
effort
drudge along like a soldier who feels no pain
pain would be better
pain would be alive, feeling something
a pin prick
a stubbed toe
so red, hot anger could rise
no
only grey
the absence
the ever-lasting fight against the all-powerful sea
i am guaranteed to lose
or maybe
i have already drowned
my head still above the water

the pendulum swings
so far in the other direction
drowning out at sea
spinning water
sucking me into its depths
swelling
i am not made for water this deep
the whales call to me
and i long for their majestic essence
to fill my heart
for me to become
one of them
but i'm drowning out here instead
and they cannot save me
the land calls to me
but on the shore
i longed to be salt-ridden
and held by the sea
i was always thirsty over there
and now i'm lost again
forgotten the feel of sand under my soles
when will i get to wade in the water?
when will i splash with abandon
knowing i am both held and free?
swimming with the starfish
whole and seen and clean?

let it be disjointed
ugly and true
you don't owe anyone your beauty

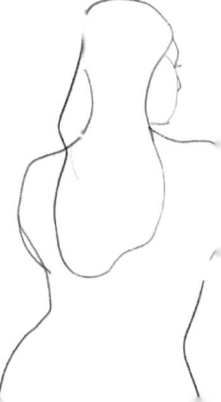

AFTERNOON ABUNDANCE

sometimes i can smell fear
on the skin of the innocent
and i can't believe
it found a way
into their bodies too

sometimes i can see anger
in the open wounds
of every daughter
and i feel sick to know
i couldn't save them

sometimes i can hear shame
in their trembling voices
and i have to trust
that they are enough
to heal themselves

sitting with uncertainty
for a time
as she reaches out her hand
and stirs my mind

i don't want to know
what's next
hold me in suspense
for nothing is more magical
than wonder and surprise

i might just sit here
and dig a while
the earth is rich under me
and i have nowhere to go
what if the treasure i seek
lies buried six feet under
or better yet
disguised as the soles of my feet?

there is a richness of us
in the depth of this forest
a texture that fills the frame
a foundation of roots growing deeper and wider
the ivy begins to wrap around us
tiny critters come to play
together we invite in a world of lost souls
to find solace in our branches

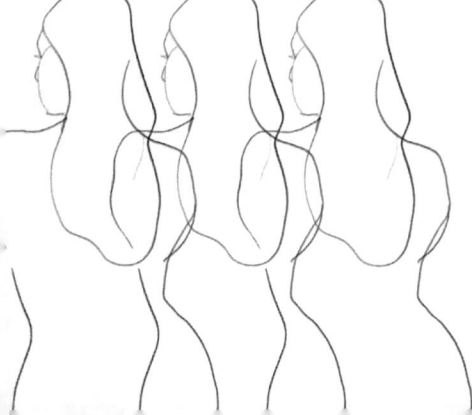

i throw myself
out into the wild world
always to come home
to you

the beast of you still looms dark in my mind
it reaches out through time and space
to knock me out of balance
just when i had forgotten
just when i got still
your sickness spread in my body
and i have been washing myself of you for years
spitting you out
scrubbing my skin
and shedding your virus
i never feel clean
i long to feel clean
like that damn spot that never comes out
you are a blood-stained mark
on my wounded mind
and i am feverishly working on the cure

do not try to tame her
or her wild mane
even if she is gone from you
she must stay free

my instinct is to banish you from my queendom
to bury you in the soil outside the grounds
for lack of time
lack of focus
lack of luster
because i know today you won't be pretty
you will let your cracks show
your wrinkles
your bags
your divots
and everyone will turn away
you are ugliness personified
and you strip me of my own beauty
i can hardly stand to look at you
you will reveal to me myself

but i cannot exile you anymore
enter my castle walls
take a seat at my table
wear my crown
you are not a guest here
you are me
and if i need to leave town
to cake myself in mud
and let you rule for a while
i will honor us both with this gift
and breathe in the modesty of you

i am sitting still
in my heart and mind
trying to find a way
to poetically say
fuck you

BLAZE

fire women of the world
made their way today
united and powerful
for a force unrecognized
i stand witness to them all
the stance of heat and love
they put the torch down
their heat is within

he bubbles up inside me
the monster of vanity
greedy and hungry
with insatiable desire
lurking in the darkness
giddy for his opportunity
to jump into the light
and scare off gentle souls
he threatens my grace
my poise, my planned nothingness
he dazzles and dances
as he eyes my plain grey overcoat
taunting me, stalking me
like a panther does her prey
the deed is already done
my whimpers add to his fun
his enjoyment of this scene
torments me
as i wish for the end of it all

then he rips me open
flooding the room with a blinding force
a rainbow explosion
excess beyond measure
i cry out in pain
for the release of my color
tears me apart
i am seen forever more
i will lose all those who are blind
but perhaps
     i will gain
          the one
               who can see

as big as you say your love for me is
you delightful fool
i am the force that surrounds it

fear of desolation
of isolation
withdrawal
will this transcend the physical form?
can i trust in the spiritual realm?
or am i taken by the past
dragged down
jolted back into the reality of my fears
dripping with guilt
fear of being seen as mother, as animal
primal and vicious and all consuming
lost to the lion in me

this two-headed monster within
shakes up my whole world
showing me once again
i am in control of nothing

we say in grief we become a shell of ourselves
why?
is it not a void from which a new force can grow?
an emptiness that must be filled with new
reborn, into greatness
the body appears the same to an untrained eye
we have not changed
but everything within us
is fresh
not simply altered
but entirely unique
we see, hear, feel and intuit
every inch of the world
as though waking for the first time
wiser, deeper
with nuance to our color
it's as if we hardly know
that human from before
i cherish her
i love her
but i do not know her anymore

to get to this beautiful
fertile place
of newness and sight
we must excavate
the self
down to the shell
sometimes it is our work
at times it is done for us
without our consent
and we stand for a moment
a shell of our former selves
bare, naked, vulnerable to the core
only from there can we rise anew
who would i be without this pain?
i cannot know her
my soul has risen too high

what if i let them float away
slowly
like a lobster in hot water
so quietly, no one even hears
the screams
so gently
like a smile to a stranger
a gift tied with ribbon
and meanwhile
i release the string
free again
to live for me

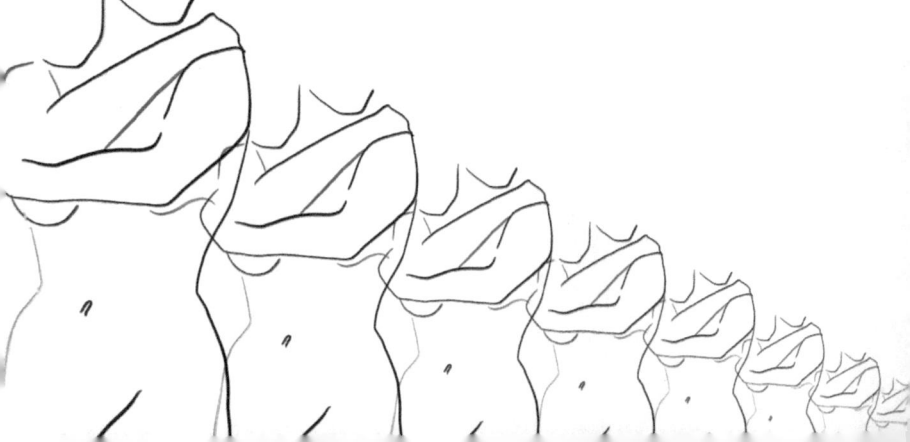

share everything
give freely
one day nothing will exist
except the stories you told
in the whispers of the night

i see your blue eyes
as they dance before me
downloading, assessing, processing
the discrepancy between my words
and my actions
you want to trust my mouth
but the wincing of my body bothers your soul
your fear gets wrapped
in a cloak of shame
eyes on you, because of me
they look, you bury yourself inside

i see your blue eyes
as they reveal the pain i have caused
by tending to myself
you reach out to heal
three tiny fingers on my hand
and i wonder
how to heal you again

you're doing it all wrong
she tells me
her teeth chomp on my skin
from the moment my eyes flutter open
she wants me underwater
where i have no power

i couldn't breathe
in this world i created
and my guilt wore me down
into nothing
trapped in this domestic web
a quicksand of mental load
labor
and split attention
i had given up countless times
and my freedom called to me
from a distant land
there is no way out but out
and i will always be behind
unfulfilled
and still
a disappointment to all

i am like blood
deep and pulsing
connected to my grandmothers
and my daughters
i spill myself into life
and death
in the same breath
many are terrified of me
they don't want to believe
that i live in them too

the beast still hangs around my coffee shop
she used to work here
barking orders at my staff
drunk with her title
and power
in such a small space
i fired her long ago
so she became an irate customer
loud and demanding
causing a ruckus
for those wanting a latte in peace
after banning her
from this establishment
she hung her head
and slunk away
i thought she was gone for good
but lately she's been peeking in the back door
hanging out in the alley
with a few choice words
for my best barista on his smoke break
somehow we must learn to co-exist
even though i want to call the cops
she would just return like a moth to a flame
so i sit here
behind the glass
and observe, coffee in hand
this sad soul
who just wants a place to call home

you try to minimize me
i am the maximum

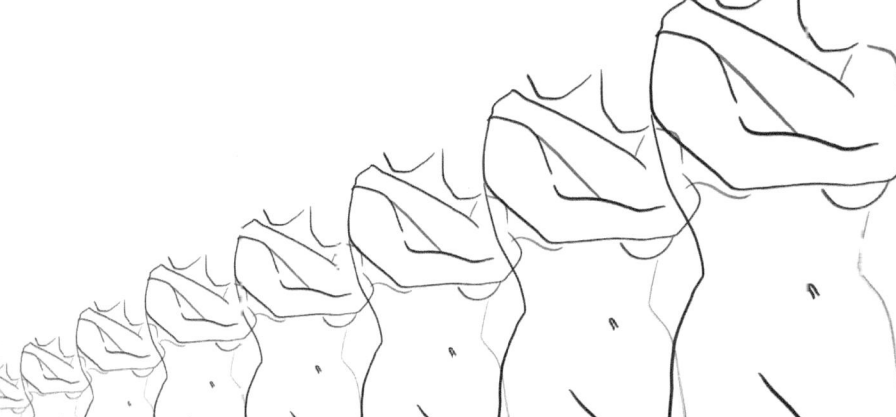

and just like that
he broke her
spilled her childhood out on the wet concrete
within a moment of knowing her
he stripped her of play
and colorful vision
she'll never say
'i love myself'
to the mirror again
please persevere
my joyful one
don't let him dim you
i pray you are brighter than me

faith
a dirty word
don't let it linger on your tongue
for long
don't let them hear you
give up your power
to something you've never seen
try not to close your eyes
and send one up
who knows where it will go
and how lost you will be
god forbid you steal a prayer
from the lips of your beloved
and ask for powers that be
to light your way
because inside your cold, dark heart
is a prison of facts
they'll keep you
caged
where you belong
believe in nothing
and you will find
nothing will get you
in the end
as you hit the ground
and return to the cold, dark earth
at least you never had
faith

how do i tear myself away
from the one who created me
rip out her imperfections
in pursuit of something greater
how do i pull this thread
and unravel the sweater
without becoming naked to the world
her cells in me and i in her
forever running from her image
and never breaking free

i pile on the layers
to comfort the wounds inside
to nourish and heat
the cells of my body
so they hurt less
i will not heal this way
not completely
but for the time being
this cocoon is how
i arrive at the next part

what is this moment of transition
feels like nothingness
empty and full of emotion
terrifying to be so lost
in the in between of spaces
my heart without a home
my feet without ground
a snail without a shell
vulnerable to the elements
naked and exposed
this feels tragic

my body is bruised
inside and out
being battered by love
and i'm staying in the ring
i will be my own demise
my opponent is fierce
intoxicating
i long for her force
to take me out
for the flutter of my eyelids
to be the last thing she and i both see
before i fall
hopeless
into the abyss of the crowd
screaming
taunting
spitting in my face
there is nowhere safe
i am beaten and broken
and one day i will rise again for more

those who shine brightly within
can be trusted to shine on you
without extinguishing their flame

all of the bal s in the air
are growing
increasing in size and scope
i look at my hands
they are the same
how will i hold them?
instead i hold my breath
as if that will help

my daughter tells me
there are three ways to pop a balloon
you can stick a needle in it
it will peter out and fall
you can let it go
into the sky
where it will pop
but no one will hear it
or you can untie it
and let the air out
right where you are

which is the best, i ask her?
well, she ponders
if you untie it
it will shrivel
but you can use it again
it still has purpose

so i inhale
knowing all will be well
if i leave the world in her hands

i bent myself towards you
as though i needed your light
out of shape
incongruent with nature
pained and hunched and efforting
i grew dry and brittle
my calloused fruit tasted bitter
i grew forgotten
no one ever remembered to pity me

why do you judge me
before i even open my mouth
i must shut out my words and thoughts
in case they misrepresent me

you dare to cloak yourself
in the costume of a false self
to sweat and bleed in the
insufferable fabric
that hides your very truth
to suffocate in the stiff dressing
that blocks your light from the world
it is wrong and stomach churning
to deprive this brave world of who you are
it quite literally makes me sick
how exhausted you must be
trapped beneath this deception
how heavy
aren't you tired?
don't you long to strip down
to your bare soul
and cleanse yourself
under the waterfall of freedom?
don't you wish to be naked and clean?
my chest burns
my mouth hangs open
at the thought
your releasing of the masquerade
the pretense
to let others see
all
of
you

i'm failing you at every turn
the distance between
who i am
and who i want to be
is an ocean of guilt
pieces of waves fall from my eyes
and the wind catches my lungs
but won't release

when it's not for me
i feel it in my chest
my heart beats erratically
warning me with heat
i am unsettled and hesitant
my body wants to bolt
the only other fighter in the ring is my mind
conniving and cunning and convincing me of lies
my eyes dart around
looking for a way out
this can't be true
it matches not the walls of my heart
the ring is noisy with opinions
logic and reason
but this heart just beats along
holding to the truth for me
exhausting to stay off the mat
to feel and deny
over and over again
my body is bruised inside and out
she cries out for relief
anywhere but here

i can't say it
it's too much to bear
but i'll spell it
one letter at a time
so my heart can pause
in between
and gather the courage
to keep beating
i'll climb this mountain
one step at a time
so my lungs don't run out of air
and i'll catch the breath
i left behind
stay with me please
i'll get there soon enough
my way

she believed she was a girl
when everyone else saw woman
she felt she got it wrong
when she oozed of all that is right
this labyrinth in her mind
was a garden to those around her
and when she finally saw all she had become
and looked back through the lens of now
the beauty of all she had ever been
bloomed before her

you are stuck in my chest
caged in by expectation
fluttering to be set free
beating on my lungs
desperate to be exhaled
and weighing me down
like the heat of summer
i have no choice
but to let you struggle
for now
and return in the light of day

i told you not to come
you weren't invited
but like a clown
creeping over a fence
to a 5-year-old's birthday party
you came right in
and everyone screamed
with delight
or fear
they don't know you but
you are curiously familiar
an archetype of fun
with the reality of crass and evil
you barged in and took over
and when i returned from the kitchen
lit cake in hands
my song was stolen
by your raspy voice
i want to scream and rip off your facade
and jerry springer you
but instead i stand in silence
frozen by your deftness
and sad that i turned my back
for only a moment
to light the candles
for the celebration of another year
of little me
when your show is over
let me know
i'll be sipping tea
and remembering
that i am the mother here

even though i've told her
that messy is beautiful
even though her knotted hair
means she's been dreaming all day
even though taking up space
is her superpower
she still thinks that to be loved
she needs to be perfect

vibration forms
on a continuum
always changing
always moving
never fully sustained
even in stillness
how strange
to never fully come to a rest

where is our village?
i watch the sad, sunken eyes of isolation
and deprivation
trod down the sidewalk
long past fatigue
and into an uncurable state
of being forgotten
gone is the vitality
the life force that channeled all of existence
to create and bring forth a soul
and all that's left
is a gaping wound
that was never stitched closed
how is it that we discard
the ultimate givers of life
tossing them to the wild animals of exile
serving them endless commodities
in a vast cardboard box
without the touch of guiding hands
and knowing hearts
every drop of wisdom and colostrum
wiped clean by a cold shipment
designed to solve an unanswerable question
where
    is
       our
          village?

'i'm missing a color'
she spoke to me
heart broken open at the sight
bleeding out her secret to me
as i held her wild mind
in the folds of my hands
'i see their palettes
with pigments i have never known'
devastated by the unfolding
of this sacred mystery
'how do i paint this world
with less than all the rest?'
she cried
and all i could see
was an artist who wanted to paint

i have found her
the queen
the one i knew
was inside me all along

this land
once was a battleground
where people were made or lost
dying in the heart
getting sucked into the abyss
gone from reality
or worse
made a hero, and then persecuted
a terrifying place
better to run far away

but with time
the world has rotated
the seasons have changed
and now this land is a playground
a bubbling colorful arena
each apparatus unique
room for all
an open invitation
to creatively play
i long to be there, expressing my joy
and art
all feelings accepted
and totally welcoming of the moment
until it turns to dust
and something new is reborn

you are a work of art
don't believe me?
live today as art itself
make each movement a dance
wear colors that emerge from your soul
choose your words like poetry
see the impact of your art
in the eyes of strangers
do this from dawn to twilight
once
and try to tell me
you are not art itself

i have no idea where you fled to
but your colors flutter around in me
they burn my throat
and fly out of my mouth
sticking themselves to others
asking 'am i a match?'
you do not blend in
i can see where the stitching comes apart
because you were not meant for this world of now
you painted the ceiling with ideals
but your feet could not be in this dirt
i don't want to f oat anyway
i would rather jump and fall
knowing the Earth will hold me
i don't know where you are
but you have no invitation here

i just realized in this circus
i am the ring leader
but i am not qualified
please don't tell anyone that i'm in charge

the water is receding
i am dry and parched
the sun burns my skin
and i wonder if i will always feel this thirsty
it feels i will be here forever
sinking deeper
and feeling so far from my dreams
just then, a glimmer of sunlight
sparkles on the film as she runs away
my eyes follow
she leads my gaze up and out
to the monstrous ocean before me
and the fortress of a wave
gaining strength in the distance
my eyes wider
my knees quake
she is coming for me
fear and excitement flood my body
they dominate me
i doubt my ability to take her on
the tsunami in my mind rains
but she is coming for me
as i glance back down
at my two bare feet
curious if they can keep me standing
i see the receding waters have buried them
giving me the foundation i need
she has prepared me for her power
and i am as ready as i'll ever be

the goddess inside me is roaring
she has been waiting for me to see
this truth, this burden
the lies we were told
she emerges from the cave
glistening
delicious but raw
her wild hair falls
knotted
and sprinkled with Earth
mud covers her torso
but the magic of her brilliance
shines through
she radiates fierce gold
as she stands
in the destruction of all i once knew
her face bears the truth
and i crumble to my knees
i cannot unsee this
i cannot unknow this
but she is with me
she is here now
her gold will save me

EMBER

send me all the broken people
send me misery and dread
send me flat on the floor
knocked out bloody and dead
i don't want to fix them
i just want to witness their broken beauty
and show them where the light shines through

she had known love before
floating, high, the wind between her ears
the exalted rush of breath
the inhale, the tears
she had known love at times
the flutter of wings
the echoes of light, dancing in the day
the space between longing and fears

she had not known the heat
searing into her skin
matching her pulse
intense and wonderful
she had not known this flame
the unstoppable power it could contain
the lingering like smoke
from a fire far away

she had not known the pull of the tide
the depth of infinite waters
held by ancient force, by waves of dark
and rich with glimmers of light
she had not known to crave the sea
the great unknown, eternal life
an ocean of curiosity that might pour forth
and fill her well of wonder

she had not felt the ground this right
a permanence rooted in truth
unshaken, untempted, stable
a history explored on this self-same soil
she had not known the lands this vast
her feet touched down
sunken in, held
here to stay until her return
to even deeper below

explosions of galaxies
in this one moment
every feeling under the sun
in this one breath
you fire out your emotions
in my direction
because i will catch them
and hold them safe

i cracked myself open
like an acorn
trying to reach the sun
bravely nudging this tender sprout
into the bold and mystic light
but my shell broke and fell to pieces
oozing my insides into the ground
crying, i frantically scooped the mush
and tried to save my soul

cover me and leave me here
gaze not upon my delicate wounds
that are exposed before you
let me wrinkle and die
on my own terms
i can live with myself
but if you find me faulty
i cannot survive

dig your hands down nto the soil
and unearth the worms
tilt your head up to the sky
and feel the sun
sit here for a while
and let it rain
before you let the moon guide you to the stars

if i could decorate these walls with words
they would be brilliantly bejeweled
of sage and sapphire, ceramic and stardust
leather bound books full of aged paper
bespeckled and blended
feathers and fallen tears
moonstones and marigold
aesthetically
available
always

the strength in me
is easy to love
my fierce lioness
has a mane
long and thick
for traveling the sahara together
you'll hear my roar
and delight in possibility
that love is effortless
i am Queen of the kingdom

but who can love
my skin and bones
when i am weak
from famine
when i have fallen
and can no longer
be the light you need?
who will hold me in the dark
and fill this senseless heart
with whispers of calm?
who can see
that my brave is still there
buried
but strong?

as you brush my matted mane
i can see
you are the one
strong enough
to hold my mess

i want to be too much
too colorful
too deep
i want to understand too much
i want to see too far
i want to be way too much for almost everyone
but just enough for you

if i asked you to detail a car
you would spray it hot pink
glue jewels to the windshield
and tie ribbons to the mirrors
you would remove the wheels
open the floor
and grow flowers through the windows
you would pop the trunk
install a victrola
and sunbathe on the roof
i would go anywhere with you
because your mind is a playground
and i am here to play

at one time
the youthful mess of you
was free
colors flying, heart wide open
limitless
where did they bury you?
you are caked in mud and heavy
the tragedy of their rules
lives in your creases and folds
come here, sweet one
i will wipe you clean

we are a gooc little team
a rough and tumble bunch of critters
we fall and cry
we repair and rise
we are carbon copies of each other
our long wild hair
and sensitive eyes
our sturdy bocies mace to carry
water
to carry life
and yet we can destroy each other
with our wicked tongues
if we forget that only we
can hold each other up

this part of me wants
to run away
and hide in the mud
where i belong
caked in earth and muck
intended isolation
so you don't see
these ugly truths

i bury myself
so your magnificent beauty
is not tainted by suffering
and the music of your heart
can fly free

i'll be here
no need for rescue
stay where you are
and let me protect you

the beast still lives in me
she doesn't lead the way
but her voice calls
from a pace behind
i am heavy knowing
she won't just go

cup of warmth
fill me with your light
the delight of my days
now freed from emptiness
shoot your beams into me
make my skin remember
the truth i once knew
lift me to the sky
as i am weightless
a feather
laughing in the breeze
ground me into the Earth
my bones crunching the leaves beneath me
the only sound i know to be true
release me to the wild
free me into the land
powered by the vast expansion
of Mother Nature
guide me to my present moment
with awe
and wonder
at the great spirit that thrives
in me
in all
as one

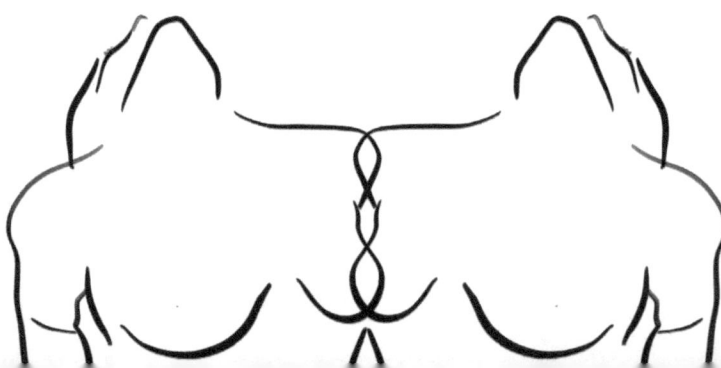

i see you more careful n this world
because of how they see you
and the lioness in me crawls out
suddenly i am your protector
because this world is not fair
we will stay in
we will not be brave
i will protect you this way
i'll lead you from there
as though it doesn't exist
sometimes we turn up
and sometimes we lay low
so lay with me here in the savannah
and i will keep watch for you

the days pass like leaves falling
each one a new color
my mind becomes blurry
trying to make sense of it all
any of it
to know is one thing, clear
to explain feels like quicksand
the words coming out wrong
misinterpreted
trying to clean it up backwards
making it worse
the more i struggle
the deeper i sink
better to wash it away
come back to myself
and remember
i'm the only place like home

everything is
confounding and wild
yet you
make perfect sense
to me

hot heat flooding
seeking cover
escape
let me be anywhere
but here
i am a child
ruinous and wrecked
punish me
so my blood
comes from everywhere
and i finally feel real

who are you to arrest my soul
and bury yourself in the deepest parts of me?

i'm ready to rip myself open
down to the core
deep and wild and raw
to feel what's beneath
like the darkness of the ocean floor
to hold big and bold and heavy water
as real as i can get
there is nothing left
on the surface for me
i belong with the whales
the bellows, the booms
the echoing in my chest
of sounds that my ears can't hear
i'll go there, i'm not afraid
i'll dive off the cliff's edge
freefalling
open to penetrate what looks like stone
where my eyes and voice are muted
and all that's left
is to feel
i'll go there, i belong there now
embodied
embraced by the inner contents
of this body
weightless yet powerful
deep and fearless
i'll go there now

i see you
you shine first within
so you have enough fire
for everyone else

the muscles of my mouth
could not control the words
from tumbling out
my body recoiled
but you held me tight
'hang on to her', your body spoke to you
the warm container of us
kept me safe
even while the dragon in my mind
breathed danger into my heart
let it be scary
for with you i have no fear
bring on the world
and i will still be home with you

this feeling
this touching of something
i can't explain
trying to put words
to matters of the soul
it fills me with
endless creativity
the joy of seeking
the never finding
always searching
thrill
because this knowing
this truth
lives inside
and the delight
of this
already exists
so we laugh
attempting to find
human words
for godly things
all the while knowing
it will never be
just right
and thank god
because then
it would be over

the moment i became unafraid of death
is when i started living
and when i realized
we are all dying in every moment
i saw the beauty in burning

your fear is beautiful
for it means you are here
do not resist your eternal transformation

how did you just bring me to the floor
with the expansion of us
flew me out of the window
heart in my mouth
trying to swallow
but i need to chew for a while
to bathe in this spring of mist
and just float
naked and free
i drink up this moment
and your desire for more connection
with me
and my extension of self
i bask
now is the perfect time to be
with me

the fire is burning, gaining strength
the branches of the tree explode in new directions
options teeter on the edge of overwhelm
stay grounded
infinite growth comes from infinite depth
roots swirling so deep, we forgot what air tastes like
from beneath, we rise infinitely
exploding in beautiful chaos
the gifts are from below
the unearthing of life
not to be repulsed by this dark soil
i am captivated by its beauty
it pulls us together
it drew me to you
and rooted in the earth
side by side
you and i, my love
we explode together

still erasing your memories
from my psyche
and it feels i will never escape
you spoil the breeze
and poison my clarity
leaving my body to burn
but this will not last
your shadow will not fall on me
or this new experience of myself
i know i am free

she was blended into me
like Cher too good for high school
as if she would let that beast
have a say in this world
he spoke too loud and too much
for too long
it's our time now
and she will silence him for good

FOSTER WILSON

she loves you so
and in that love
she has separated her and i
mother and daughter
there is now a part of her
i will never understand
my flesh and blood
part of her heart
no longer mine

i feel heavy with the weight of this burden
losing all sense of myself
wishes and fantasies vanished
along with showers and sleep
i regret everything
then feel guilty for that
time just pours out of me
fun disappears
and i'm still just tending to everyone else
what the hell happened
to me?

i cannot believe the days keep coming
without end
churning and turning like a treadmill
we have to keep feeding our mouths
and our souls and our babes
no wonder some are being dragged
by the collar
of life
sunken eyes and road rash
undernourished
and forgotten by the sun
everyone needs to eat the light

i need to express my mess
in less beautiful ways
tormented by perfection
and novelty
i continue to have fewer answers
so what am i telling you for
i'll just be this pile of shredded organs
and let you stitch together
meaning from my leftovers

it felt like a dream dashed
slashed with a knife
guts spilling out of the curtain
onto the floor in a single mess
knocking our great love
down into lesser territory
until these wounds scab over
new skin forms and i realize
we are meant for more
more of everything
more space, more life
more colors, more freedom
more novelty, more connection
more appreciation, more presence
more closeness, more fire
more strength and understanding
that only we
have the secret
and the power
and the intention
and the magic
of it all

everything we know is a lie
there is no path
the marigold blocks lead us
right into an inescapable well
we are spokes of a wheel
infinite choices
infinite directions
colorful and creative
we forgot our everything

you'll find me in a puddle on the floor
fallen from the release of truth from your lips
weak from disbelief
even though nothing could be more true
to know i am the one you adore

i don't want to be in the next town over
describing the landscape to you
calling you over to this village
for the best wine and cheese
i want to be just one breath ahead
far enough to scan the horizon
for creeks and rocks
close enough to hold your trembling hand
and let you wander off
please promise
you will do the same for me
as soon as you are able

if you are angry with me
slam the door
i will slip a note under it
telling you how much i adore you
you will tear it up
because that is your job
and that's how i know
you love me

we were a trilogy
a perfect set
a trifecta of the feminine
wild and free
arms linked
and safe together
then you came
and wrapped a blanket around us
showed us the laughter
that was already there
you became the chair
for us to stand on
and i can see
when one of us needs
to venture off
for a bit
you can keep the light on
and the space warm
for somehow
this is exactly
what we needed
and exactly what was meant for you

with the weight of the sun
heavy on my eyelids
i drifted off to rest
you covered my chest with your book
and became my shade
protecting my fair skin
from too much of a good thing
for you are my sun
and my shade
in the same breath
and i thrive freely
being watered by you

we are the wild ones
with the story no one will believe
naked and free
screaming the truth from within
the woods echoing our bodies
beating the drum of the spirit
our minds left far behind
impulsive, running, leaping
arms stretched wide
and voices broad and booming
a volume that is effortless
and grand
the laughter of freedom
the wet and lush desire
of life being lived
thrilled to have a voice
and a body, two
with which to leap
this essence, this heartbeat
it all comes down
to you
my wild one
set free into the jungle
the beyond
with me

when left alone
your delightful colors
shine infinitely

inside
the light of you
pours through the cracks
as it pierces your skin
deeper and deeper
until you are naked
and yet not afraid
for the world wants you as their cake
and you my dear
are the sun

immerse me in art
cover me in color
massage me with music
form me into expression itself
where i will happily drown

your mumblings amuse me
creative genius at work
source flowing through you
as a discovery
the perfect process
the sounds still forming
never still
ever changing
surrendering to the moment
knowing there is no end
and creation
is magic

strip away all the color
down to its essence
in monochrome, the details emerge
the simplicity stuns
and the soul is given the mic
and just when the air has calmed
and the exhale is complete
EXPLODE me with pigment
fuchsia, marigold, turquoise and violet
flood my senses
and overwhelm my lungs
with all the brilliance this world has to offer
show me a palette without words
so i can die happy in the bed
of life's exuberance

you forgot you were an artist
but i'm looking at your art
you are creating in every moment
painting the world around you
accidentally
let your paint splatter on my skin
for i want to be canvas and collector
in the same breath

the stars want to explode from your eyes
and pierce the veils around you
the colors want to escape from your chest
and run wild through the streets
your blood pumps with desire
for knowing and seeing all there is
the jewels burst from your mouth
in your thirst for everything
and you're terrified of this power
what words can i say
to help you feel safe
to keep the floodgates open
to be as big and bold as you are
because just as the world craves your colors
you are also dying to let them free

yes, you truly are so much
and quite actually
so
much
more

i see you falling
deeper and deeper
into awakening
closing your eyes
to feel the sun
and seeing more clearly this way
the warmth of my body
melting your fears
and bringing calm
to your mind
it is pure delight
to watch you discover
what i have known
all along
that we will walk through this world
shoulder to shoulder
heads high and hearts open
receiving all this gold
that life has to offer

this is me
showing up for the party
gold-encrusted gown
peacock feathers six feet in every direction
bejeweled frames the size of montana
big and bold in every way
spilling over in excess
fabulous
flawed
flying
i've unlearned everything i was taught
and now the party can begin

sun flooding your face
hand in mine
breath in the air
to know in the moment
this will be something we remember

GRATITUDE

I pour my well of grat tude into the Earth...

...to all my readers, known and unknown, for opening your
heart to new colors

...to my parents for seeing the artist in me always

...to my children for lighting my creative spirit

...to my brother for your deep loyalty

...to my illustrator ard designer, Suz Born, for your
generosity and delightful collaboration

...to my fellow creatives: Jennica Schwartzman, Samara Bay,
Jamaal D. Pittman and Glenn Milley, for being a collective
of guiding lights in this process

...and to my partner, Cesar Cardona, for your boundless
inspiration, infinite wisdom and deeply-rooted belief in my
abundance. You are my sun and shade in every breath.

ABOUT THE AUTHOR

FOSTER WILSON is a creative nurturer of magical things, weaving her artistry into film, photography, poetry, and birth work. Her career in film spans two decades, both in front of and behind the camera. Foster's award-winning films include *Made Public*, *Waffles and 5 Stages of Grief*, where she effortlessly blends off-beat humor and dynamic characters with cinematic integrity.

Her poetry started as a private journey of self-exploration, born out of messy journals and early morning musings, exploring themes of love, loss, motherhood and the yearning for a more vibrant life. Her artistic endeavors are deeply personal, seeking connection and understanding with the human experience in all its messy beauty. Foster's nurturing spirit extends to the birth world, empowering birthing people in their postpartum experiences.

She is a contributor to *The Drill Mag* and holds a BFA from New York University's Tisch School of the Arts.

www.fosterwilson.com
@thefosterwilson